Twitter Bootstrap Web Development How-To

A hands-on introduction to building websites with Twitter Bootstrap's powerful front-end development framework

David Cochran

BIRMINGHAM - MUMBAI

Twitter Bootstrap Web Development How-To

First published: November 2012

Production Reference: 1121112

Published by Packt Publishing Ltd.
Livery Place
35 Livery Street
Birmingham B3 2PB, UK.

ISBN 978-1-84951-882-6

www.packtpub.com

Cover Image by William Kewley (william.kewley@kbbs.ie)

Credits

Author

David Cochran

Reviewers

Chris Gunther

Veturi JV Subramanyeswari

Acquisition Editor

Sarah Cullington

Commissioning Editor

Meeta Rajani

Technical Editor

Vrinda Amberkar

Project Coordinator

Michelle Quadros

Proofreader

Maria Gould

Production Coordinator

Melwyn D'sa

Cover Work

Melwyn D'sa

About the Author

David Cochran is Associate Professor of Communication at Oklahoma Wesleyan University. He and his students have a fondness for envisioning and producing exciting projects, with well-built standards-compliant websites playing a central role in them. David frequently publishes online tutorials to share insights gained in the course of those projects. In recent months, Twitter Bootstrap has been a key topic. You'll find a number of these tutorials at `Webdesign.tutsplus.com` and at his blog, `aLittleCode.com`.

I would like to thank my wife, Julie, and our kids. Thanks for riding through the busy times with grace. And thank you for the joy you bring. I'm grateful beyond words.

I would also like to thank my colleagues, students, and former students at Oklahoma Wesleyan University. You make learning and teaching a pleasure. I look forward to many more projects together.

About the Reviewers

Sree (aka **Veturi JV Subramanyeswari**) is currently working as a solution architect at a well known software consulting MNC in India. After joining this company she served a few Indian MNCs, many start ups, R&D sectors in various roles such as programmer, tech lead, research assistant, and architect. She has more than 8 years of working experience in web technologies covering media and entertainment, publishing, healthcare, enterprise architecture, manufacturing, public sector, defense communication, and gaming. She is also well a known speaker who delivers talks on Drupal, Open Source, PHP, women in technology, and so on.

She has also reviewed other technical books such as *Drupal Rules*, *DevOps*, *Drupal 7 Multi Sites Configuration*, *Building Powerful and Robust Websites with Drupal 6*, *Drupal 6 Module Development*, *PHP Team Development*, *Drupal 6 Site Blueprints*, *Drupal 6 Attachment Views*, *Drupal E-Commerce with Ubercart 2.x*, *Drupal 7: First Look*, and *Drupal SEO*.

> I would like to thank my family and friends who supported me in completing my reviews on time with good quality.

Chris Gunther is the co-founder of Room 118 Solutions, a web development consultancy based out of the New York. Chris is a web application developer, handling both frontend and backend development. He has contributed to many open source projects, including Bootstrap. Chris spends most of his time developing with Ruby on Rails.

www.PacktPub.com

Support files, eBooks, discount offers and more

You might want to visit www.PacktPub.com for support files and downloads related to your book.

Did you know that Packt offers eBook versions of every book published, with PDF and ePub files available? You can upgrade to the eBook version at www.PacktPub.com and as a print book customer, you are entitled to a discount on the eBook copy. Get in touch with us at service@packtpub.com for more details.

At www.PacktPub.com, you can also read a collection of free technical articles, sign up for a range of free newsletters and receive exclusive discounts and offers on Packt books and eBooks.

http://PacktLib.PacktPub.com

Do you need instant solutions to your IT questions? PacktLib is Packt's online digital book library. Here, you can access, read and search across Packt's entire library of books.

Why Subscribe?

- ▶ Fully searchable across every book published by Packt
- ▶ Copy and paste, print and bookmark content
- ▶ On demand and accessible via web browser

Free Access for Packt account holders

If you have an account with Packt at www.PacktPub.com, you can use this to access PacktLib today and view nine entirely free books. Simply use your login credentials for immediate access.

Table of Contents

Preface

One of the joys of front-end web development is its culture of spontaneous generosity. Run into trouble achieving your desired design? Is browser X or Y causing you problems? Chances are someone has identified the problem, worked out a solution, and posted it with a demo and code samples. Google it up, tweet a thanks, post a comment, maybe even donate a buck, and you're fast friends on the road to some serious web design conquests.

Over the years this basic disposition has scaled itself up. From icon packs and gradient generators to grid systems and GitHub projects, our profession's culture of generosity has grown in sophistication. Need a great grid, thoughtful typography, expertly crafted buttons? Perhaps some user-friendly form elements? Can do. Here, there, and yonder, you'll find a plethora of tips, tools, and packs to get it done.

It's a beauty to behold.

Generosity meet cohesion!

Yet perhaps you've noticed an unintended consequence of this habitual generosity. The proliferation of tips, tools, recommendations, and solutions emerge from all across the web. When solutions come from every which way, things can become a bit chaotic. A certain amount of cohesion and consistency are important to design, including interface design. And yet cohesion and consistency often seem to be among the scarcest of resources on the Web. Not that this problem is a new one. The industry of mobile application design handles it by providing developers with Software Development Kits (SDKs) that include carefully honed, cohesive approaches to addressing the standard needs of interface design. The industry of web design, by contrast, has typically not enjoyed the widespread use of similar front-end development kits.

Not, that is, until Twitter Bootstrap.

When Twitter developers Mark Otto and Jacob Thornton first released Twitter Bootstrap in August 2011, they made a splash. Understandably so, as their framework supplied carefully crafted yet easily modified styles and scripts for the essential elements of a complete web interface. In January of 2012, Twitter Bootstrap 2.0 brought a number of enhancements, most significantly a responsive layout which adapted to desktops, tablets, and handhelds. Thus it has happened that, as of this writing, Twitter Bootstrap has quickly become the most watched of all GitHub projects, with more than 33,000 Github users watching it—more than twice the closest runner up. To emerge so quickly from a field of contenders which includes the likes of the HTML5 Boilerplate and the jQuery JavaScript library, this is no small feat. Given the rate of its growth and the size of its community, we may be forgiven for suspecting that we have something serious on our hands.

A serious community

Like the HTML5 Boilerplate and the jQuery library, Twitter Bootstrap represents an informed and energetic community exerting its best efforts toward a common and shareable set of best practices. Without demanding submission or commanding uniformity, the community exerts authority for a simple reason: it produces a cohesive collection of tested, tried, and proven lines of code. The code base may be adopted and embraced, customized and modified, or dissected and examined. In all cases it offers serious solutions for real problems—solutions that speed developers on their way to serving up consistent, reliable, and user-friendly web experiences.

The proof is in the pudding. Visit a few of the many sites collected at BuiltwithBootstrap.com `<http://builtwithbootstrap.com>` and you'll find a pleasing variety of designs sharing a few key features in common: strong typographical conventions, a well formed grid, and a user-friendly interface, amply endowed with cross-browser compatibility and multi-device friendliness to spare. Many a developer has achieved these results without the aid of Twitter Bootstrap, of course, but there is little doubt that Bootstrap helps the cause and contributes to a better Web. Adopt it wholesale or dissect and inspect it, we stand to benefit from the transaction.

What this book covers

Downloading and setting up (Must know), walks you through the basics—getting the CSS, images, and JavaScript, and creating a page template.

Headings, links, and buttons (Must know), introduces you to Bootstrap's ready-made styles for clear typographic hierarchy and turning hyperlinks into visually appealing buttons.

Conquering the layout (Must know), experiments with Bootstrap's fantastic twelve-column grid system, just to get familiar with it.

Creating a standard sub-page (Must know), applies the Bootstrap grid system to lay out a standard sub-page with a wide main column and a narrower sidebar.

Creating a portfolio page (Must know), assists you in laying out a full-page grid of linked images with captions, using Bootstrap's styles for thumbnails.

Creating a products page (Must know), walks you through the steps involved in creating a products page. Bootstrap comes with effective styles for laying out a good, basic, visually appealing table. We'll use it to start a products page.

Customizing the navbar (Must know), assists you in adding links to these pages in Bootstrap's main navigation bar.

Making it responsive (Should know), connects jQuery and Bootstrap's JavaScript plugins to enable the navbar to adapt responsively to small devices and viewports.

Adding drop-down lists (Should know), shows how to add drop-down lists to your navbar. With the JavaScript in place, it's quite simple.

Using tabs for switching content (Should know), illustrates the use of tabs for switching content. Now that we're getting used to leveraging all of Bootstrap—markup, CSS, and JavaScript—we're ready to create dynamic tabs for switching between panes of content.

Creating a homepage carousel (Should know), adds a final touch to your site. To finish our site, we'll add a beautiful image slideshow, using Bootstrap's excellent, fully responsive carousel.

Optimizing and customizing (Should know), will show you how to optimize your site for better performance and how to add customizations. Out-of-the-box Bootstrap is great. But you'll want to customize it. We'll bring in some custom colors and font faces. And we'll optimize our files in the process.

Uploading, testing, and launching (Must know), walks you through a basic process of uploading our site to the web. Then you'll leverage a couple of great online tools to test our site for both desktop and mobile devices.

Appendix: Bootstrap resources, contains a list of resources to help you continue growing as a Bootstrap-equipped developer.

What you need for this book

The requirements are pretty simple: a computer, an Internet connection, a text editor, and a desire to learn!

Who this book is for

I've written with the novice to intermediate developer in mind. If you're new to HTML, CSS, and JavaScript—don't worry! I'll help you along. If you've been designing sites for a while, the book is an ideal way to get a quick introduction to Twitter Bootstrap's distinctive markup, CSS, and JavaScript plugins. If you're an advanced developer, interested in customizing Bootstrap and working with LESS to preprocess your CSS, I'm afraid this book is not for you!

Conventions

In this book, you will find a number of styles of text that distinguish between different kinds of information. Here are some examples of these styles, and an explanation of their meaning.

Code words in text are shown as follows: "Rename the file `index.html`."

A block of code is set as follows:

```html
<div class="hero-unit">
  <h1>Hello, world!</h1>
  <p>This is a template ...</p>
  ...
</div>
```

When we wish to draw your attention to a particular part of a code block, the relevant lines or items are set in bold:

```html
<div class="item active">
  <img src="img/butterfly.jpg" alt="butterfly" />
<div class="carousel-caption">
<p>Caption content here</p>
</div>
</div>
```

New terms and **important words** are shown in bold. Words that you see on the screen, in menus or dialog boxes for example, appear in the text like this: "Click on the large **Download Bootstrap** button".

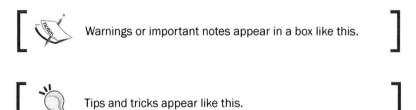

Warnings or important notes appear in a box like this.

Tips and tricks appear like this.

Reader feedback

Feedback from our readers is always welcome. Let us know what you think about this book—what you liked or may have disliked. Reader feedback is important for us to develop titles that you really get the most out of.

To send us general feedback, simply send an e-mail to feedback@packtpub.com, and mention the book title via the subject of your message.

If there is a topic that you have expertise in and you are interested in either writing or contributing to a book, see our author guide on www.packtpub.com/authors.

Customer support

Now that you are the proud owner of a Packt book, we have a number of things to help you to get the most from your purchase.

Downloading the example code

You can download the example code files for all Packt books you have purchased from your account at http://www.PacktPub.com. If you purchased this book elsewhere, you can visit http://www.PacktPub.com/support and register to have the files e-mailed directly to you.

Errata

Although we have taken every care to ensure the accuracy of our content, mistakes do happen. If you find a mistake in one of our books—maybe a mistake in the text or the code—we would be grateful if you would report this to us. By doing so, you can save other readers from frustration and help us improve subsequent versions of this book. If you find any errata, please report them by visiting http://www.packtpub.com/support, selecting your book, clicking on the **errata submission form** link, and entering the details of your errata. Once your errata are verified, your submission will be accepted and the errata will be uploaded on our website, or added to any list of existing errata, under the Errata section of that title. Any existing errata can be viewed by selecting your title from http://www.packtpub.com/support.

Piracy

Piracy of copyright material on the Internet is an ongoing problem across all media. At Packt, we take the protection of our copyright and licenses very seriously. If you come across any illegal copies of our works, in any form, on the Internet, please provide us with the location address or website name immediately so that we can pursue a remedy.

Please contact us at `copyright@packtpub.com` with a link to the suspected pirated material.

We appreciate your help in protecting our authors, and our ability to bring you valuable content.

Questions

You can contact us at `questions@packtpub.com` if you are having a problem with any aspect of the book, and we will do our best to address it.

Twitter Bootstrap Web Development How-To

Welcome to *Twitter Bootstrap Web Development How-To*. The content of this book is up to date with version 2.1 of Twitter Bootstrap. In what follows, this book will help you to get to know **Twitter Bootstrap** by trying it on for size. I've written with the novice to intermediate developer in mind. If you've been designing sites for a while, then this book will give you a quick introduction to several key features of Twitter Bootstrap's markup, stylesheets, and JavaScript plugins. If you're new to HTML and CSS (and maybe even a little scared of JavaScript)—don't worry! This book will help you along. If, by contrast, you're looking to compile CSS from LESS and integrate the results with Backbone.js—this isn't for you.

Fair enough?

Let's dive in.

Downloading and setting up (Must know)

In a few simple steps, we'll put together a basic starter site equipped with Twitter Bootstrap's framework of stylesheets, icons, and JavaScript plugins.

Getting ready

Twitter Bootstrap is more than a set of code. It is an online community. To get started, you will do well to familiarize yourself with Twitter Bootstrap's home base:

```
http://twitter.github.com/bootstrap/
```

Here you'll find the following:

▸ **The documentation**: If this is your first visit, grab a cup of coffee and spend some time perusing the pages, scanning the components, reading the details, and soaking it in. (You'll see this is going to be fun.)

▸ **The download button**: You can get the latest and greatest versions of the Twitter Bootstrap's CSS, JavaScript plugins, and icons, compiled and ready for action, coming to you in a convenient ZIP folder. This is where we'll start.

Downloading the example code

You can download the example code files for all Packt books you have purchased from your account at http://www.PacktPub.com. If you purchased this book elsewhere, you can visit http://www.PacktPub. com/support and register to have the files e-mailed directly to you.

How to do it...

Whatever your experience level, as promised, I'll walk you through all the necessary steps. Here goes!

1. Go to the Bootstrap homepage: http://twitter.github.com/bootstrap/.

2. Click on the large **Download Bootstrap** button.

3. Locate the download file and unzip or extract it. You should get a folder named simply bootstrap. Inside this folder you should find the folders and files shown in the following screenshot:

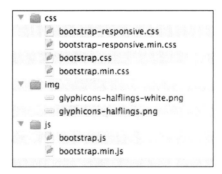

4. From the homepage, click on the main navigation item: **Get started**.

5. Scroll down, or use the secondary navigation, to navigate to the heading: **Examples**. The direct link is:

```
http://twitter.github.com/bootstrap/getting-started.
html#examples
```

6. Right-click and download the leftmost example, labeled **Basic Marketing Site**. You'll see that it is an HTML file, named `hero.html`.

7. Save (or move) it to your main bootstrap folder, right alongside the folders named `css`, `img`, and `js`.

8. Rename the file `index.html` (a standard name for what will become our homepage).

   You should now see something similar to the following screenshot:

9. Next, we need to update the links to the stylesheets.

   Why? When you downloaded the starter template file, you changed the relationship between the file and its stylesheets. We need to let it know where to find the stylesheets in this new file structure.

10. Open `index.html` (formerly, `hero.html`) in your code editor.

Need a code editor?

▶ **Windows users**: You might try **Notepad++** (`http://notepad-plus-plus.org/download/`)

▶ **Mac users**: Consider **TextWrangler** (`http://www.barebones.com/products/textwrangler/`)

11. Find these lines near the top of the file (lines 11-18 in version 2.0.2):

```
<!-- Le styles -->
<link href="../assets/css/bootstrap.css" rel="stylesheet">
<style type="text/css">
  body {
    padding-top: 60px;
    padding-bottom: 40px;
  }
</style>
<link href="../assets/css/bootstrap-responsive.css" rel="stylesheet">
```

12. Update the `href` attributes in both `link` tags to read as follows:

```
href="css/bootstrap-responsive.css"
```

13. Save your changes!

You're set to go!

Open it up in your browser! (Double-click on `index.html`.)

You should see something like this:

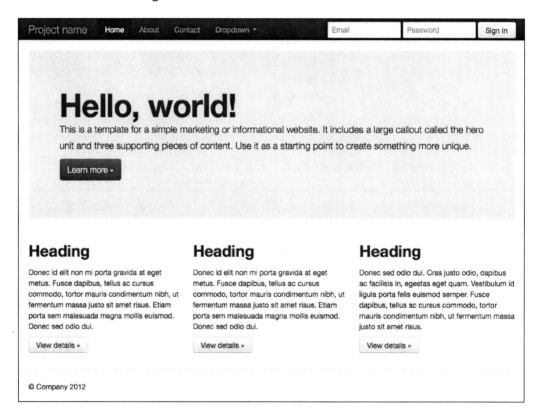

Congratulations! Your first Bootstrap site is underway.

Problems? Don't worry. If your page doesn't look like this yet, let me help you spot the problem. Revisit the steps above and double-check a couple of things:

▸ Are your folders and files in the right relationship? (see step 3 as detailed previosuly)

▸ In your `index.html`, did you update the `href` attributes in both stylesheet links? (These should be lines 11 and 18 as of Twitter Bootstrap version 2.1.0.)

There's more...

Of course, this is not the only way you could organize your files. Some developers prefer to place stylesheets, images, and JavaScript files all within a larger folder named `assets` or `library`. The organization method I've presented is recommended by the developers who contribute to the HTML5 Boilerplate. One advantage of this approach is that it reduces the length of the paths to our site assets.

Thus, whereas others might have a path to a background image such as this:

```
url('assets/img/bg.jpg');
```

In the organization scheme I've recommended it will be shorter:

```
url('img/bg.jpg');
```

This is not a big deal for a single line of code. However, when you consider that there will be many links to stylesheets, JavaScript files, and images running throughout your site files, when we reduce each path a few characters, this can add up. And in a world where speed matters, every bit counts. Shorter paths save characters, reduce file size, and help support faster web browsing.

Headings, links, and buttons (Must know)

If you're familiar with HTML, you'll quickly be able to size up the sample content provided in our `index.html` (formerly `hero.html`). But there are a few Bootstrap-specific opportunities that I'll raise to your attention.

Getting ready

If you're new to HTML, then let me point you to some assistance. The excellent HTML tutorials and references at `http://htmldog.com` will help you get up to speed quickly. The HTML Beginner Tutorial will equip you with the baseline essentials, though I would encourage you to work through intermediate and advanced versions as well. Additionally, I would strongly encourage you to work through the corresponding CSS tutorials, as you'll gain a much better understanding of the fundamentals behind Twitter Bootstrap. Then come back and continue!

HTML Dog
The Best Practice Guide
To XHTML and CSS

HTML Beginner Tutorial

This **HTML Beginner Tutorial** assumes that you have no previous knowledge of HTML or CSS.

If you're familiar with HTML (or once you've tackled these tutorials), take a moment to note the headings and the class `hero-unit`. We'll do some further customization using our own headings.

With `index.html` opened in your editor, scroll down to approximately line 76, where you'll find the `h1` heading, `<h1>Hello, world!</h1>`. Scrolling on down, you'll see a couple of `h2` headings at lines 84, 89, and 94, roughly. (Note that the precise line numbers and some elements may change in future versions of Twitter Bootstrap.)

Observe that headings get considerably larger when nested inside the `div` of class `hero-unit`. Back up around the first `h1` heading, you'll see the following tag structure:

```
<div class="hero-unit">
  <h1>Hello, world!</h1>
  <p>This is a template ...</p>
  ...
</div>
```

The `hero-unit` class calls in Bootstrap CSS rules that scale up font sizes, creating a welcome message that can't be missed. You'll note that things aren't too large outside the `hero-unit` in the headings and paragraphs below.

Now it's time to customize your own content!

How to do it...

1. Edit the `h1` heading, and add a `<small>` tag within it. Edit the text to read as follows, adding `small` tags in the mix as follows:

    ```
    <h1>Welcome to my site! <small>I think you'll like it.</small></h1>
    ```

2. Save the file, then view it in your browser (and refresh the page if needed).

You'll see that Bootstrap styles the text between the `small` tags in a way that creates what we might call a pseudo-subheading.

Welcome to my site! I think you'll like it.

When needed, you can provide similar `<small>` pseudo-subheadings within all headings, `h2` through `h6`. (See `bootstrap.css` for styles for `h1 small`, and others.). This is one of the many small touches that makes Twitter Bootstrap so fun to use.

We can also turn links into buttons. Let's note how easy it is to turn a standard link into a button in Twitter Bootstrap.

1. Viewing `index.html` in your editor, scroll down below the comment, `<!-- Example row of columns -->` and look under the sample h2 heading and paragraph.

2. You'll find the following. Be sure to notice the class:

   ```
   <p><a class="btn" href="#">View details &raquo;</a></p>
   ```

   In your browser the result is a very respectable looking button!

   The class `"btn"` does the magic! (If you'd like, search `.btn` in `bootstrap.css` to see the relevant styles.)

3. Experiment with these related button classes.

4. Now scroll back up `index.html` in your editor to find the sample link inside the `div` class `hero-unit`, and notice the classes used for this link:

   ```
   <p><a class="btn btn-primary btn-large">Learn more &raquo;</a></p>
   ```

   The `btn-primary` class gives this button its blue color, and `btn-large` increases its size. (Again, you may search to find the relevant lines of CSS in the `bootstrap.css` stylesheet.)

There are more pre-built sizes and colors available, which you should take a few minutes to experiment with. Available classes include the following:

▶ Colors:
   - ❑ `btn-primary`
   - ❑ `btn-info`
   - ❑ `btn-success`
   - ❑ `btn-warning`
   - ❑ `btn-danger`
   - ❑ `btn-inverse`

▶ Sizes:
   - ❑ `btn-large`
   - ❑ `btn-small`
   - ❑ `btn-mini`

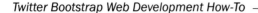

You can find these and other available styles documented in Twitter Bootstrap's documentation pages at `http://twitter.github.com/bootstrap/base-css.html#buttons`.

How it works...

As you have begun to see, Twitter Bootstrap provides a number of handy styles to meet the needs of many frequently occurring circumstances—including some style options that you may not have considered before but that could be useful to you! If you've not read carefully through Twitter Bootstrap's online documentation, be sure to do so.

In addition, you will learn a great deal by opening the `bootstrap.css` file and reading through it yourself. Grab a cup of coffee, break the task into manageable chunks of time, and tackle a few lines. You'll become more familiar with how Twitter Bootstrap works. And if you run across something that's new to you, you can research it and build up your own knowledge base as a bonus.

There's more...

When you're ready, you can build your own customized color scheme using Twitter Bootstrap's excellent **Customize** page, found in their documentation at:

`http://twitter.github.com/bootstrap/customize.html`

Once there, you will see options to customize a number of things. If you'd like to focus primarily on the color scheme, scroll down to the appropriate section—**Customize Variables**. Update the color variables with your desired values, and click on the large **Customize and Download** button at the bottom to get your customized version of Bootstrap! Customization will be important, as it will help you to distinguish your site from the many other Bootstrap sites out there.

First things first, however. Before we start innovating, we need to get familiar with the fundamentals. Next up, we'll experiment with page layout using Twitter Bootstrap's excellent grid system.

Conquering the layout (Must know)

One of the persistent problems of web design is achieving an effective, cross-browser compatible layout. Over the years, some excellent frameworks have been developed to tackle this problem. Twitter Bootstrap features a variation on the popular 960 grid system (see it at `http://960.gs/`). By comparison, Bootstrap's grid system offers a simpler syntax. It is also responsive, so that the layout can adjust to devices of varying sizes, from desktop computers to tablets and handheld devices.

Soon we'll use this grid system to create a few new pages for our custom site. First, let's get familiar with the basic features of the Bootstrap grid system.

Getting ready

Let's begin by creating a page that we'll use as a "Layout Playground".

1. Create a copy of `index.html`, and name the new file `layout.html`. (Make sure this new file is in the same folder as `index.html`.):

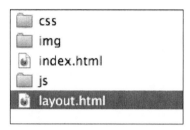

2. Open `layout.html` in your code editor.

3. Customize the content of the `title` tag, so that you may easily recognize this file when it's open in your browser. Make it read something similar to the following code. (Note that I've used the pipe symbol, which you should find above the return or *Enter* key on your keyboard—*Shift* + \ (backslash). This is not absolutely necessary, however.)

```
<title>Layout Playground | My Bootstrap Site</title>
```

4. Also customize the content of the `h1` heading, to read similarly. (You'll find this heading at approximately line 59, inside the `div` tag of the `hero-unit` class).

```
<!-- Main hero unit for a primary marketing message or call to
action -->
    <div class="hero-unit">
        <h1>Layout Playground</h1>
```

5. Open `layout.html` in your browser. You should see the content and layout, as shown in the following screenshot, in the area below the top navigation:

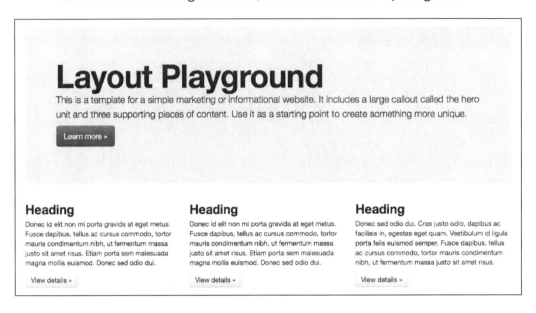

Your playground is ready! Time to start having some fun.

How to do it...

We won't experiment with every possibility right now. (Let's save some fun for future steps!) But we'll take a few minutes to experiment with some of the basic options for setting up rows with columns of varying widths.

1. In `layout.html`, find the comment which reads `<!-- Example row of columns -->`. (This should be at line 64, approximately.)

2. Beneath that, you'll find these lines:

```
<div class="row">
        <div class="span4">
```

3. Scan on down, and you'll notice that there are two more `div` tags with `class="span4"`. We're going to adjust these span classes to adjust the widths of these three columns.

4. Change the first `span4` to `span6`, and the second and third to `span3`:

```
<div class="row">
  <div class="span6">
  ...
  <div class="span3">
```

```
. . .
<div class="span3">
. . .
```

5. Save the file and refresh your browser. The left column should grow wider, and the second and third columns should be narrower, as shown in the following screenshot:

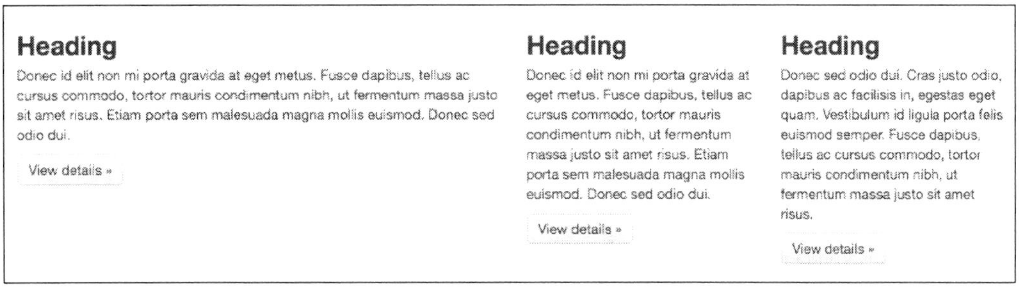

6. Now let's make a new row and lay it out differently! In your editor, scan further down the file to the `<hr>` tag just before the `<footer>` tag. Above this, locate the last closing `</div>` tag. This is the end of the example row. Add a comment as follows:

```
</div><!-- end .row -->
```

7. Select the entire row and its contents (all lines including `<!-- Example row of columns -->` through `<!-- end .row -->`).

8. Copy this content by either navigating to **Edit | Copy**, or pressing *Ctrl + C* (on a PC) or *cmd + C* (on a Mac).

9. Paste the new row just after the current one.

10. Change the span classes in the new row so that they read as follows:

```
<div class="row">
    <div class="span2">
    . . .
    <div class="span4">
    . . .
    <div class="span6">
    . . .
```

11. Remove roughly two-thirds of the paragraph text from the `div class="span2"`.

12. Save the file. Refresh your browser, and you should see something very much like the following!

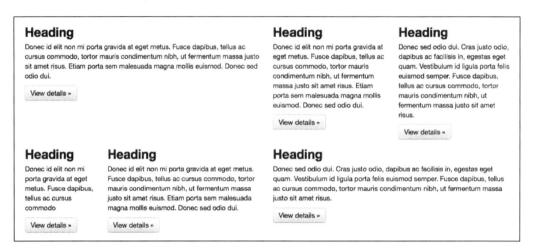

13. If your results are different, take a few minutes to review the previous steps and troubleshoot. For instance, you might double-check to make sure that you pasted your new row after the closing `div` tag for the original row.

```
</div><!-- end .row -->

<!-- Example row of columns -->
<div class="row">
...
```

14. Now take a few minutes to experiment on your own, creating new rows, new columns, and experimenting with span values. Knock yourself out! If your results get out of whack, don't worry! This is a playground. You've got rubber flooring and padded equipment. No permanent damage will be done. Play around. We'll leave the playground and do some serious work soon enough.

How it works...

Twitter Bootstrap uses a 12-column grid system. Thus, its span values run from 1 through 12. `span12` is full-width, `span8` is two-thirds, `span6` is half width, and so on. The `div class="row"` is built to contain a row of columns. Each new row creates a new zone for laying out columns as desired. (If you're familiar with floats and clearfixes, the columns float left and the row includes a clearfix to ensure that the columns don't get tangled.)

There's a lot of power available in this system. We'll be leveraging some of that power in our next steps. But feel free to visit Twitter Bootstrap's documentation under the **Scaffolding** section to learn more:

`http://twitter.github.com/bootstrap/scaffolding.html`

And of course you'll want to open `bootstrap.css` and check out the stylesheet rules yourself! Open the file in your editor, and search for `.row` or `.span` to find the relevant rules.

There's more...

If you're using a modern browser (Internet Explorer 9 or a recently updated version of Mozilla Firefox, Google Chrome, Opera, or Safari), resize your browser window. Make it narrower, then narrower still. You should see that the grid system adjusts to fit!

As of version 2.0 (released late January 2012), Twitter Bootstrap comes with the principles of responsive web design built into its grid system. This is documented on Bootstrap's Scaffolding page, mentioned previously. You'll find the media queries that make this happen in the `bootstrap-responsive.css` file.

If you're concerned about users with old browsers, don't worry. Browsers that don't understand media queries will simply get the standard 960-pixel-width version. One of the things that makes Twitter Bootstrap such a dependable tool is that it combines powerful, cutting-edge features with the time-tested principles of progressive enhancement and graceful degradation.

Creating a standard sub-page (Must know)

Now that we're familiar with the basics of the Bootstrap's grid system, we can start creating pages for our first Bootstrap website. Let's start with a standard sub-page with a main column and sidebar. We'll make it our "About" page.

Getting ready

Let's get our new template file ready:

1. Make a copy of `index.html` and rename it `about.html`.
2. Open `about.html` in your editor.
3. Update the `title` tag to read `<title>About | My Bootstrap Site</title>`.
4. Update the `h1` heading to read `<h1>About this Site</h1>`.
5. Save the file and open it in your browser.

Now let's get down to business.

How to do it...

1. Inside the `div class="hero-unit"`, beneath the `h1` heading, delete the two paragraphs (including the contained text and button). We're going to turn this `h1` tag into a basic page header.

2. Update the class of `div class="hero-unit"` so that it reads `div class="page-header"`. Rather than a large messaging unit, the styles for class `"page-header"` give us a nice page title.

3. Save the file, and refresh your browser. You should see a result like this:

4. Now, inside the `div class="row"`, look for the first `div class="span4"`. Change it from `span4` to `span8`. We're going to use this for our wide main column.

5. Delete the entire next `div class="span4"` and its contents. We're not going to need this column.

6. Save the file, and refresh your browser. You should now have a two-thirds-wide left column and one-third-wide right column.

About this site

Heading

Donec id elit non mi porta gravida at eget metus. Fusce dapibus, tellus ac cursus commodo, tortor mauris condimentum nibh, ut fermentum massa justo sit amet risus. Etiam porta sem malesuada magna mollis euismod. Donec sed odio dui.

View details »

Heading

Donec sed odio dui. Cras justo odio, dapibus ac facilisis in, egestas eget quam. Vestibulum id ligula porta felis euismod semper. Fusce dapibus, tellus ac cursus commodo, tortor mauris condimentum nibh, ut fermentum massa justo sit amet risus.

View details »

© Company 2012

Now we have a template for a two-column page, ready to be filled with main content on the left and sidebar content on the right.

Let's keep going just a little bit more, so that we have a better picture for what might be done with such a page.

7. Let's add a large introductory image to our main column. You can use one of the following methods:

 ❑ **Method A**: Use a local image. Take any image of your choice, edit it to 600 px wide, and place it in the `img` folder. Name it `about-image.jpg`. (I've assumed it's `jpg`, but of course you can adjust this for `png` or `gif` formats.) Place a `img` tag just before the `h2` heading in your `div class="span8"`.

 ```
 <img src="img/about-image.jpg" />
 ```

 ❑ **Method B**: Use a placehold.it image. Alternatively, you may use the handy service, `placehold.it`. Visit `http://placehold.it` and read its instructions to see how the service works. In this case, your image link will work like this:

 ```
 <img src="http://placehold.it/600x300" />
 ```

8. Now let's make some adjustments to the sidebar. Repeat Method A or B , as outlined previously, to add a 300 pixel wide image before the heading inside your `div class="span4"`.

9. Change the sidebar `h2` heading to a `h3` heading, as it is subordinate to the previous heading.

10. Give the sidebar some additional content by selecting the heading, paragraph, and button, and copying and pasting it below.

11. Save the file, and refresh your browser. I've used placehold.it images. Here is my result:

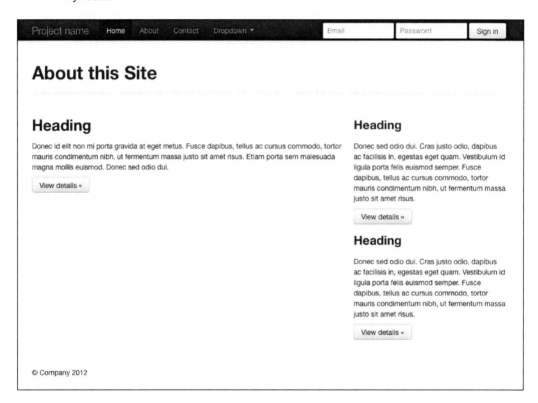

 If your results aren't what they should be, look back over your steps, checking for unclosed tags or other errors. If you're new to web design, don't be afraid to start from scratch and repeat the process. You'll get faster with practice, and soon you'll get used to spotting errors more quickly.

If your results look more or less like mine, congratulations!

There's more...

If you're using a modern browser, resize your browser window. Make it narrower, and then narrower again. Notice that not only do the columns adjust their widths to fit your window—the images adjust to fit as well!

An essential part of a responsive web design is that it provides CSS rules to keep images from overflowing the width of their containers. Thus, you'll find this rule in `bootstrap.css`:

```
img {
    max-width: 100%;
    ...
}
```

While we're at it, take a moment to look again at Twitter Bootstrap's Scaffolding documentation, and scan on down the page. Notice that if you need more space between columns, you can add a class of `offset`. Moreover, you can nest rows and columns, enabling you to place a row of two narrower columns inside your large main column. If you would like your columns to be entirely fluid, using percentage widths instead of pixels, you can use the class `row-fluid`. The possible combinations are nearly endless.

Creating a portfolio page (Must know)

Soon we will update the navigation bar to provide links to the pages we're creating. First, let's create two more pages. Next up, a portfolio page.

In this page, we'll place more emphasis upon images. To speed things up as we learn, we'll use placehold.it images, together with Twitter Bootstrap's handy styles for thumbnails, so that we may quickly organize a grid of images with headings and captions.

Getting ready

Let's get our new template file ready:

1. Make a copy of `about.html` and rename it `portfolio.html`.
2. Open `portfolio.html` in your editor.
3. Update the `title` tag to read `<title>Portfolio | My Bootstrap Site</title>`.
4. Update the h1 heading to read `<h1>Portfolio</h1>`.
5. Save the file and open it in your browser.

How to do it...

1. Our portfolio page will be full-width, with no sidebar. Therefore, we need to remove the sidebar, `div class="span4"`.
2. Now adjust the main column to fill the entire width. Change its class from `span8` to `span12`.

3. Use a placehold.it image to provide an image wide enough to stretch to the full width of the site. Replace the former 600 pixel wide image with 1200 pixel wide placehold. it image, shown as follows:

```
<img src="http://placehold.it/1200x400" />
```

Save the file and refresh the browser. The image should stretch the full width of the site container.

In a modern browser, take a moment to resize the browser window to make it narrower. As in the About page, so here, the image will scale down as the width of the site scales down.

4. Leave the heading, paragraph, and button, as if these describe the currently featured portfolio item. Below these, after the closing tag for `div class="row"`, we will add a grid of subordinate items.

5. We'll use a thumbnail grid to lay out two rows of four thumbnail images each. To do this we'll create a special unordered list, of class `thumbnails`, to provide the markup to lay out our grid. Start with this markup:

```
<ul class="thumbnails">
<li class="span3">
     <div class="thumbnail">
        <a href="#">
           <img src="http://placehold.it/300x200" alt="" />
        </a>
        <h4>Item Label</h4>
     </div><!-- .thumbnail -->
   </li><!-- .span3 -->
</ul>
```

Note that we've opted for a fairly complex version of the thumbnail system. Each thumbnail is wrapped in a list item, and the thumbnail class is applied to a div, which serves as a container for a linked image and a label. In addition, we are controlling the width of the thumbnail by applying a class of `span3`.

6. Copy the list item and its contents, and create seven additional copies, creating a total of eight thumbnails.

7. Save the file, refresh, and look at your result. Here is mine:

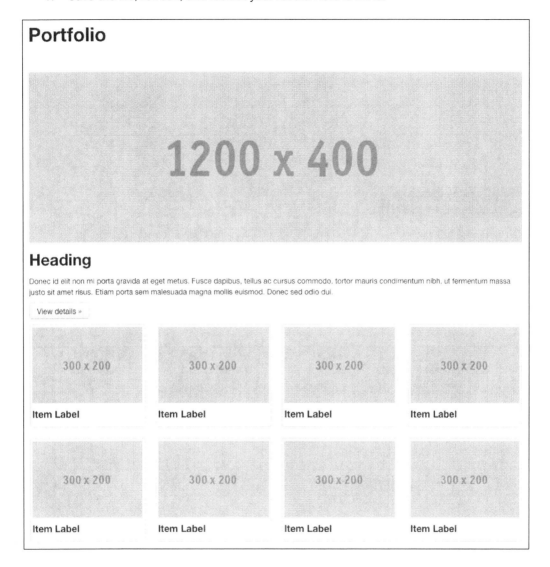

Creating a products page (Must know)

Before we finish creating pages, let's quickly create a basic products page with columns and rows for products, prices, and features.

Getting ready

Let's get our new template file ready for our products page.

1. Make a copy of `about.html`, and rename it `products.html`.
2. Open `products.html` in your editor.
3. Update the `title` tag to read `<title>Products | My Bootstrap Site</title>`.
4. Update the `h1` heading to read `<h1>Products</h1>`.
5. Save the file and open it in your browser.

How to do it...

We're going to create a basic table template for laying out features of products.

1. In the page, we'll use a narrow left-hand sidebar for an introduction to our table. Update the column div `class="span8"` by changing the `span8` to `span3`, and update the contents of the h2 heading to say something more descriptive, such as, "What we have to offer."
2. Update the second column to become a wider column with a class of `span9`.
3. Replace the contents of the second column with the following table tag with associated classes:

    ```
    <table class="table table-striped table-bordered">
    </table>
    ```

4. Next add a table head row and headers, with the following markup:

    ```
    <thead>
      <tr>
        <th>Heading</th>
        <th>Heading</th>
        <th>Heading</th>
        <th>Heading</th>
        <th>Heading</th>
      </tr>
    </thead>
    ```

5. Following the table head, start a table body with a beginning row:

    ```
    <tbody>
      <tr>
        <td>Info</td>
        <td>Info</td>
        <td>Info</td>
    ```

```
        <td>Info</td>
        <td>Info</td>
     </tr>
  </tbody>
```

6. Copy the table row and its contained cells (everything including and between the tr tags), and make four additional copies directly beneath the first row and within the tbody tags.

7. Save the file and refresh your browser. My results look like this:

Products

What we have to offer	Heading	Heading	Heading	Heading	Heading
	Info	Info	Info	Info	Info
	Info	Info	Info	Info	Info
	Info	Info	Info	Info	Info
	Info	Info	Info	Info	Info
	Info	Info	Info	Info	Info

Donec id elit non mi porta gravida at eget metus. Fusce dapibus, tellus ac cursus commodo, tortor mauris condimentum nibh, ut fermentum massa justo sit amet risus. Etiam porta sem malesuada magna mollis euismod. Donec sed odio dui.

© Company 2012

Thus, in short, you have a nice-looking table ready to be customized to your specific needs.

Customizing the navbar (Must know)

Twitter Bootstrap's main navigation is organized in the **navbar**. In this recipe, we'll begin our first steps in customizing the navbar by creating links to our new pages. For those of you experienced with HTML, this will not be difficult, but we can begin noting interesting features of the navbar along the way!

Getting ready

1. Open `index.html` in your editor.

2. Update the document title tag to read `<title>Home | My Bootstrap Site</title>`.

3. Scroll down just below the opening `body` tag (line 35, approximately) where you'll find the markup for the navbar, which begins with the following tag:

```
<div class="navbar navbar-fixed-top">
```

You're there!

Take a moment to scan through approximately the next 18 lines of code, and you'll see that the navbar is composed of nested divs, links, and lists, with special classes. These classes serve significant purposes, from positioning and styling to setting up the responsive navigation.

I'll briefly summarize the roles of these classes:

▸ `navbar` provides the outside containing element for all contents of the navbar.

▸ `navbar-inverse` calls for a dark navbar background with light font color.

▸ `navbar-fixed-top` fixes the navbar at the top of the window and lets page content scroll underneath it (this requires padding at the top of the body element. See it in the embedded style sheet in the head of the `index.html` file.)

▸ `navbar-inner` provides height, padding, and background color and gradients.

▸ `container` constrains the width of the navbar contents, centers them within a wide screen, and includes a clearfix so that it will contain floated child elements.

▸ The link tag of class `btn btn-navbar` provides a button that is hidden via CSS in a wide viewport but which appears in narrower viewports, where it serves as a trigger for drop-down access to the main menu items.

▸ The div of class `nav-collapse` serves as the containing element for the menu items which are dropped down in narrow-viewport navigation.

▸ The `ul` tag of the `nav` class contains the main navigation links which take a user to various pages in a site. This is the region where we'll first start to work!

If you search for these classes in the `bootstrap.css` file, you'll find the corresponding stylesheet rules.

Now that you have the basic picture, let's start customizing.

How to do it...

1. Let's begin by creating the navbar link to our homepage. Look for the link `<a class="brand" ...>` and update its `href` value and the link text as follows:

```
<a class="brand" href="index.html">My Bootstrap Site</a>
```

2. Update the list items inside of `ul class="nav"` so that they link to the pages in your site, adding an additional list item and link for the products page. The result should look as follows:

```
<ul class="nav">
  <li class="active"><a href="index.html">Home</a></li>
  <li><a href="portfolio.html">Portfolio</a></li>
  <li><a href="products.html">Products</a></li>
  <li><a href="about.html">About</a></li>
</ul>
```

Note that `class="active"` on the `Home` navigation item provides the darkened background color which indicates the current page.

3. Save the file. Open `index.html` in your browser. The navbar should look like this:

Test the navigation links, and you should find that it takes you to the appropriate page!

You'll also find that you have to use your browser's **Back** button to get back.

It's time to update the navbar in our other pages!

4. In `index.html`, select and copy everything from `<a class="brand"` ... `>` through `<!--/.nav-collapse -->`. (This should be nine lines.)

5. Open the `about.html` file in your code editor. Select the corresponding section of code (everything from `<a class="brand"` ... `>` through `<!--/.nav-collapse -->`). Paste the updated code from `index.html` over the top of it.

6. Cut and paste `class="active"` from the `Home` list item to the `About` list item. These two list items should now look as follows:

```
<li><a href="index.html">Home</a></li>
<li class="active"><a href="about.html">About</a></li>
```

7. Save `about.html`, and open it in your browser. You should see the updated navbar with About indicated as the current page, like this:

8. Repeat the same process with `portfolio.html` and `products.html`.

9. You should now be able to navigate back and forth between your site pages, and the proper page should be marked as current.

10. Take a celebratory coffee break! We're about to have some more fun.

Making it responsive (Should know)

One of the truly exciting things about Twitter Bootstrap is that since version 2.0, its navbar adjusts responsively to small viewports such as tablets and handheld devices. At these narrow widths, the navbar cleverly adjusts to allow users quick access to the main site content, while providing a button which triggers a drop-down panel containing the main navigation items.

Getting ready

If you're using a modern browser, you can see the responsive navbar in action on your computer. With one of the site pages open, drag the window width narrower. You'll see the transformation happen when the viewport shrinks below 980 pixels wide.

Assuming you've been following the above steps, you'll find that the navbar drop-down panel is not yet functional. Click on the right-hand side button to test it.

What we're lacking is the JavaScript necessary for the drop-down behavior. Now is a good time to get the JavaScript hooked up! (We'll soon be using other JavaScript touches that come with Twitter Bootstrap's JavaScript plugins as well.)

How to do it...

1. Open `index.html` in your editor.

2. Scroll down to the bottom of the page and look for the section of code that begins with this comment:

```
<!-- Le javascript
================================================== -->
```

3. Below that comment you'll see roughly 15 lines of code, including links to `js/jquery.js` and a dozen other JavaScript files. Just as we had to update the links to the CSS files, we also need to update the links to the JavaScript files.

4. Let's start with the first, the link to jQuery. Notice that your `js` folder does not currently contain a file named `jquery.js`. Open a new browser window and navigate online to `http://jquery.com`. Find the **Download** button on the homepage and click on it. (Your browser window will fill with code—the file contents—or it may invite you to download the file.) Save the file (the file source only) to the `js` folder.

5. Update the jQuery link with the name of the downloaded jQuery file. In my case, it looks like this:

```
<script src="js/jquery-1.7.2.min.js"></script>
```

6. Below this line are Bootstrap's JavaScript plugins, each in a separate file. Our Bootstrap download, by contrast, includes all plugins compiled together into one file. You'll find it in the `js` folder—`bootstrap.js` and its minified version, `bootstrap.min.js`. We need only to link to one of these files. Let's use the minified version, as it will load faster in our users' browsers.

7. Edit one of the Bootstrap JavaScript links so that it reads as follows:

```
<script src="js/bootstrap.min.js"></script>
```

8. Delete the links to the other Bootstrap plugins, as we have them all rolled into one file.

9. Your resulting JavaScript links should look something like this:

```
<script src="js/jquery-1.7.2.min.js"></script>
<script src="js/bootstrap.min.js"></script>
```

That's it. Just two lines!

10. Save the file and refresh the page in your browser. The navbar should now drop down when you click on the button.

11. Now it's time to fix the JavaScript links in our other pages. Copy your new JavaScript links from `index.html` and use them to update the links in `about.html`, `portfolio.html`, and `products.html`.

12. Save the files, open them in your browser, and test to make sure that the drop-down menu works in all pages.

Adding drop-down lists (Should know)

While we're working on the navbar we should add a drop-down list. As drop-down functionality draws upon the same Bootstrap JavaScript plugins we connected in the previous recipe, everything is in place to make it work. We just need to add the markup.

Getting ready

1. Open `index.html` in your editor.

2. Scroll down to the `<div class="navbar ..." >` just after the opening `<body>` tag.

We're ready to start to work.

How to do it...

1. Within the `div class="navbar ..."`, find `div class="nav-collapse"`. This is the region of the navbar which collapses when the viewport width is narrower than 980 px.

2. Within this, find the unordered list `ul class="nav"`. This is where we created our custom links to our site pages.

3. We're going to create a new unordered list, `ul class="nav"` right next to this one, immediately after it and before the closing tag `</div><!--/.nav-collapse -->`.

4. Add a new `<ul class="nav">` and its closing `</ul>` tag.

5. Nested inside of this, we'll add a special list item whose purpose will be to contain the drop-down menu: `<li class="dropdown">` and its closing `</li>` tag. As the text for this list item, put `Your Account`.

   Your result should look like this so far:

```
<ul class="nav">
  <li class="dropdown">
    Your Account
  </li>
</ul>
```

6. Now to insert our drop-down items, create a new unordered list with the class of `"dropdown-menu"`, nested within the `li class="dropdown"` like this:

```
<ul class="nav">
  <li class="dropdown">
  Your Account
        <ul class="dropdown-menu">
          <li><a href="#">Login</a></li>
          <li><a href="#">Profile</a></li>
          <li><a href="#">Cart</a></li>
        </ul>
  </li>
<ul>
```

   We're almost there. What remains is to add the tag structure needed to make "Your Account" function as a drop-down trigger.

7. Wrap the text **Your Account** in a link tag with a # for its href value.

 The # for the href value is essential to the functioning of our drop-down menu.

```
<a href="#">Your Account</a>
```

8. We need to add a special class and a data-attribute to turn this link into a drop-down toggle. Let's add those:

```
<a href="#" class="dropdown-toggle" data-toggle="dropdown">Your
Account</a>
```

Save the file. Refresh the page in your browser. Click on our link and you'll see that the drop-down menu now works!

9. To add a visual cue for our users to identify the menu item as a drop-down, Bootstrap uses a b tag with a special class. Just after **Your Account** and before the closing </ a> tag, add this. Notice we'll leave a space before the <b.

```
Your Account <b class="caret"></b>
```

It should now do this for you!

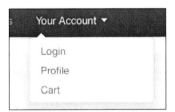

10. Finally, let's move our new dropdown menu to the right-hand end of the navbar. Bootstrap has a built-in class for this—pull-right. Add that class like this:

```
<ul class="nav pull-right">
  <li class="dropdown">
. . .
```

Save, refresh, and your dropdown menu should now be positioned at the right end of the navbar.

11. Copy your new dropdown menu to your other pages!

How it works...

If you consult the `bootstrap.css` file, you'll see how these components work. The `dropdown-menu` of the `ul` class is hidden (`.dropdown-menu { ... display: none; ... }`) until the link of `dropdown-toggle` is clicked and the JavaScript adds the `open` class to the parent list item (`.open .dropdown-menu { display: block }`).

There's more...

Take time to read through Bootstrap's documentation on the navbar and drop-down lists. You can find it here:

`http://twitter.github.com/bootstrap/components.html#navbar`

You'll find options for adding dividers, icons, and more!

Using tabs for switching content (Should know)

We've been getting familiar with implementing Bootstrap's JavaScript behaviors. Let's keep it going by adding a tabbed content switcher, as follows:

These are great for allowing users to switch briskly between items within one bounded content area. Let's add one of these to our Products page!

How to do it...

In the following steps, we'll first prepare our content and then wrap it in the appropriate tag structure to present it in a tabbed form. First let's add the content.

1. Open `products.html` in your browser. Beneath the table, we're going to add a new row with a tabbed panel **Options**. To speed our progress, we'll duplicate the entire row that contains the table and replace the table with our new content.

2. Open `products.html` in your editor and scroll down to the opening tag for the div class row, which should be at line 73, approximately:

```
<!-- Example row of columns -->
    <div class="row">
```

Click to place your cursor on the line above these lines of code.

3. Now, using your mouse, scroll down past the table with its `<td>` and `<tr>` tags until you reach the `<hr>` and `<footer>` tags. Holding down the *Shift* key, click on the line in between those two tags. You should now have a selection that includes the entire row and its contents down through and including the `<hr>` tag. (If this didn't work, try to get that selection using your preferred method!)

4. Copy and then paste a duplicate of these lines just below the `<hr>` tag and above the `<footer>` tag. Save and refresh your browser to see if you've created an exact duplicate. Now we'll update the heading on the left and replace the second table with new content.

5. In your new second row, update the `h2` heading, **What we have to offer,** to read simply **Options**.

6. Now inside the following `<div class="span9">` select and delete the entire table, including the `<table></table>` tags and everything in between.

7. Now let's grab some content to fill the space left by the table. Copy the `h2` heading and paragraph from `<div class="span3">` and paste it where the table used to be.

8. Update the heading of the newly copied text to `Option 1`. Then update its enclosing tags from `h2` to `h3`, as `Option 1` is subordinate to `Options`.

9. Let's add a placeholder image after the heading and before the paragraph:

```
<img src="http://placehold.it/400x200" alt="placeholder"
class="pull-right thumbnail" />
```

The `pull-right` class will float the image to the right. The `thumbnail` class will add a nice bit of padding and border around it.

Refresh to see your results.

10. Now make two additional copies of the `h3` heading `Option 1`, the image, and paragraph, pasting them immediately below. Update the succeeding headings to `Option 2` and `Option 3`. To make the content distinct for each, delete a line or two from the top of each succeeding paragraph, and modify the widths of the succeeding placehold.it images to 440 px and 480 px respectively.

Save the file. Refresh your browser, and you'll see the contents for what will become three switchable panes in our tabbed content switcher. To get the rest of the way there, we'll need to add some additional markup to demarcate three distinct panes of content and to supply the tabs to switch between them.

11. First, we need to wrap each of our three options and their content within a div of the `tab-pane` class. Before each `h3` heading, add `<div class="tab-pane">`. Then close each of these tab-panes with a closing `</div>` tag after each corresponding paragraph.

12. For our switching tabs to work, each of these panes will need a distinct ID. Add an ID to Option 1's opening tag, so that it reads like this:

```
<div class="tab-pane" id="option1">
```

Do the same for the next two panes, giving them IDs as `option2` and `option3` respectively.

13. Next wrap these three panes together within a single containing `<div class="tab-content">`, which should begin before `option1`'s opening tag and then be closed with a `</div>` tag placed after `option3`'s closing `</div>` tag.

14. Save the file. Refresh your browser and you'll see that all of the content disappears. That's good! The panes of content are hidden until triggered by their respective tabs. But of course we want the first pane to appear by default. We need to add a class of "active" to the first pane.

```
<div class="tab-pane active" id="option1">
```

Save and refresh again, and you'll see this pane return to view!

15. Now the tabs. These begin as a simple unordered list with two special classes—`nav`, which marks it as a navigation list, and `nav-tabs`, which will call in Bootstrap styles to render the list items to look like tabs. Add these lines immediately after `<div class="span9">` and before `<div class="tab-content">`.

```
<ul class="nav nav-tabs ">
  <li>Option 1</li>
  <li>Option 2</li>
  <li>Option 3</li>
</ul>
```

16. These list items now need to be wrapped as page anchors, each linking to its respective tab pane's ID. Thus the first list item should be wrapped as follows:

```
<li><a href="#option1">Option 1</a></li>
```

Do the same with the others, using `#option2` and `#option3` for the `href` values. Save and refresh your browser. You'll see the tabs appear above the tab content, sort of. Notice that they don't really look like a tab until hovered over.

17. We need to mark the first tab as the active tab by default. Add the `active` class to its `li` tag, like this:

```
<li class="active"><a href="#option1 "...
```

Save, refresh, and you'll see it receives the styles of a current tab!

18. We're almost there. At present, our tabs do nothing when clicked. We need to tell Bootstrap's JavaScript to do its magic here. This requires adding a data attribute to each tab's link tag, like this:

```
<a href="#option1" data-toggle="tab">Option 1</a>
```

Be sure to add the same attribute to the other two tab links as well.

Save. Refresh. Click your tabs. See your panes. High five!

There's more...

The fun needn't stop here! Take a moment to visit the **Nav: tabs, pills, and list** section of Bootstrap's Components documentation at:

```
http://twitter.github.com/bootstrap/components.html#navs
```

You'll see that Bootstrap provides several options for positioning and styling the navs and pills, simply by adjusting classes on key elements. Be bold. Try out some creative variations. Have some fun. Grow your palette of design possibilities in the process!

Creating a homepage carousel (Should know)

Bootstrap abounds with well-built JavaScript plugins. We can't possibly introduce them all here. But let's choose another of the more popular ones—the carousel plugin—to enhance our homepage with a sliding carousel of content and images. Such carousels are very effective at giving users a visually attractive overview of what a website is about. We've seen them. We want one. Bootstrap has it ready for us.

Getting ready

In this exercise, we'll replace the homepage's large welcome message with a carousel, using Bootstrap's built-in styles and JavaScript.

Start by lining up sample images for your carousel. If you'd like, you may use the images provided with the files for this exercise, which you will find in the _Carousel Images folder. You'll see that these are sized and cropped to equal dimensions—1200 px wide by 480 px high. These dimensions will provide a pleasing ratio while allowing the images to stretch to the full width of our site on a widescreen monitor.

We'll be replacing hero-unit in index.html with our new carousel. Before we do that, let's make a backup copy, so that we'll have a template file that contains hero-unit with its large welcome message. Make a copy of the index.html file and name it hero.html. With the images ready and the backup copy preserved, we're set to go.

How to do it...

We are going to work in `index.html`, first adding the markup for our images and then adding the additional markup and a bit of JavaScript to enable the carousel.

1. Open `index.html` in your editor.

2. Delete the entire `div class="hero-unit"` and all of its contents.

3. Copy or move the images for your carousel to the `img` folder. We'll use the `img` folder for all images used in our web pages.

4. In place of `hero-unit`, place image tags for each of your images. Include `alt` attributes. To enhance the responsiveness of our images to adapt to multiple screen widths, leave out the width and height attributes.

   Your resulting code should look like this so far:

   ```
   <img src="img/butterfly.jpg" alt="butterfly" />
   <img src="img/colors.jpg" alt="colors" />
   <img src="img/galaxies.jpg" alt="galaxies" />
   <img src="img/jupiter.jpg" alt="jupiter" />
   ```

   Save the file. Open it in your browser, and you should see four large images displayed one after the other. Now let's add in the markup structure to turn the images into items in our carousel.

5. Wrap two containing `div`s around the entire set of images, as follows:

   ```
   <div class="carousel" id="home-carousel">
     <div class="carousel-inner">
       <img … />
       <img … />
       <img … />
       <img … />
     </div><!-- .carousel-inner -->
   </div><!-- .carousel -->
   ```

6. Next wrap each image in its own `div` of class `"item"`:

   ```
   <div class="item">
     <img src="img/butterfly.jpg" alt="butterfly" />
   </div>
   ```

   Be sure to do the same for each image.

   Save the file and refresh your browser. You will see that the images have disappeared entirely! That's because the styles for these elements serve to hide all except for the currently active item.

7. Add the `active` class to the first image:

```
<div class="item active">
```

Now save and refresh, and you'll see the first image—and only the first image—appears! We're a step closer. But of course our carousel needs to start cycling from one image to the next. This requires some JavaScript.

8. We need to initialize Bootstrap's carousel plugin to do its magic in our page. Scroll down the page to just before the closing `</body>` tag. After the script links to jQuery and Bootstrap's JavaScript, add the highlighted lines:

```
<script src="js/jquery-1.7.2.min.js"></script>
<script src="js/bootstrap.min.js"></script>
        <script>
          $(document).ready(function(){

            $('.carousel').carousel();

          }); // end document.ready
        </script>
```

This script does two things:

- ❏ `$(document). ready(function()` waits until our document is ready for manipulation in the browser
- ❏ `$('.carousel').carousel();` tells the Bootstrap carousel plugin to do its work on our div of the `carousel` class

 If you wanted to give your carousel container a different class, of say `"super-slider"`, you'd adjust this line to read: `$('.super-slider').carousel();`

After providing these lines, save the file and refresh your browser. Watch it for five seconds, and you should see it switch (suddenly, with no animation) to the next image—and continue to cycle to the next image each five seconds.

 Hovering your mouse over the images will pause the cycling.

9. Now let's add sliding animation. This is very simple. Add the `slide` class to the parent `div` of `class="carousel"`, like so:

```
<div class="carousel slide" id="home-carousel">
```

10. Next, let's add the Next and Previous arrows. Add the following lines between the closing div tags for `carousel-inner` and `carousel`:

```
</div><!-- .carousel-inner -->
  <a class="carousel-control left" href="#home-carousel" data-slide="prev">&lsaquo;</a>
  <a class="carousel-control right" href="#home-carousel" data-slide="next">&rsaquo;</a>
</div><!-- .carousel -->
```

 It's important that the `href` value references the `id` given to the outermost parent `div` of our carousel. We've given it the `id` "`home-carousel`", and we've made these match.

Save the file, refresh in the browser, and you should see Next and Previous arrows at each end of your slideshow image!

11. Now how about adding a caption to our images? Here's how it's done:

```
<div class="item active">
  <img src="img/butterfly.jpg" alt="butterfly" />
      <div class="carousel-caption">
        <p>Caption content here</p>
      </div>
</div>
```

The paragraph tag is required, as it calls in the light text color to contrast clearly against the caption background. You'll find sample caption content in the `_Carousel Images/credits-captions.txt` file.

Repeat for all four images. Save, refresh, and you should see a result like this:

Congratulations! You've successfully implemented one of the more complex and exciting of Bootstrap's JavaScript plugins.

There's more...

Be sure to consult Bootstrap's carousel documentation to learn more, including options for tweaking the settings. Feel free to experiment!

Having conquered drop-downs, tabs, and the carousel, you are ready to experiment with Bootstrap's other excellent plugins. Set aside a couple of hours, consult the excellent documentation and examples, and give them a try.

Optimizing and customizing (Should know)

It's almost time to take this website online. Let's get things ready by optimizing our files for better performance. While we're at it, we'll customize a few key design elements to begin making the design our own.

An optimized website loads faster. It reduces unnecessary load on your web server. And it helps improve your ranking in major search engines. We can't cover all aspects of site optimization in this brief book, but we can take two steps that will make a big difference:

- Trimming down our CSS and JavaScript files by removing unused code
- Using the minified versions of the CSS and JavaScript files

Bootstrap provides a great tool to help us get this done.

It also provides options for quickly customizing several key design features. We'll take a moment to customize our headings' font and the color scheme of our navbar.

How to do it...

Let's begin by trimming out unused portions of our CSS and JavaScript. We could do it line by line, and there are tools that could help with that. But the **Customize** page in Bootstrap's documentation helps us do a respectable job with much greater time efficiency.

1. Go to Twitter Bootstrap's documentation, and navigate to the **Customize** page: `http://twitter.github.com/bootstrap/customize.html`.

2. Note the subtitle of the section titled **1. Choose components** This section allows us to select only the CSS modules we need. Uncheck the checkboxes for the features we are not using in our website. I've done this as follows:

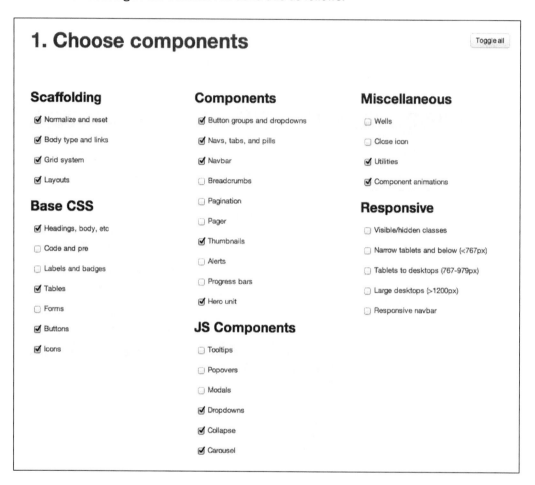

Note that I have deselected all options under **Responsive**. The responsive layout styles we need are already provided in our originally downloaded `bootstrap-responsive.css` file. What we're building here is a new, trimmed-down version of `bootstrap.css`.

3. Moving on down the page, let's build a trimmed-down version of Bootstrap's JavaScript file. Select the components, as shown in the following screenshot:

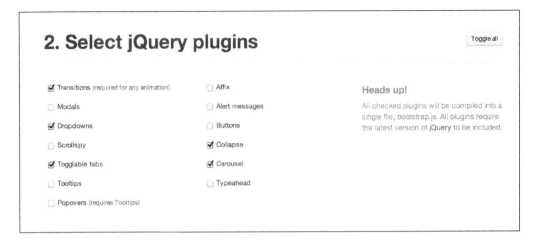

4. Now move down to the section labeled **3. Customize Variables**. Here we'll take a moment to update a few key variables.

5. In the center column under **Typography**, update the `@serifFontFamily` variable to a Palatino font family: `'Palatino Linotype', Palatino, Georgia, serif`.

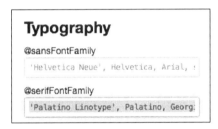

6. Now to make this the new font family for our headings, move down the same column to update the `@headingsFontFamily` variable to use the `@serifFontFamily` variable we've just specified:

Next to give your navbar a dark blue gradient. Under **Navbar** in the right-hand column, update the values for `@navbarBackground`, `@navbarBackgroundHighlight`, `@navbarText`, `@navbarLinkColor`, `@navbarLinkColorHover`, `@navbarLinkColorActive`, and `@navbarLinkBackgroundHover`, as shown in the following screenshot. (These variables and their values control the background gradient, the navbar text color, the background color for hover states, and the background for the active nav item.)

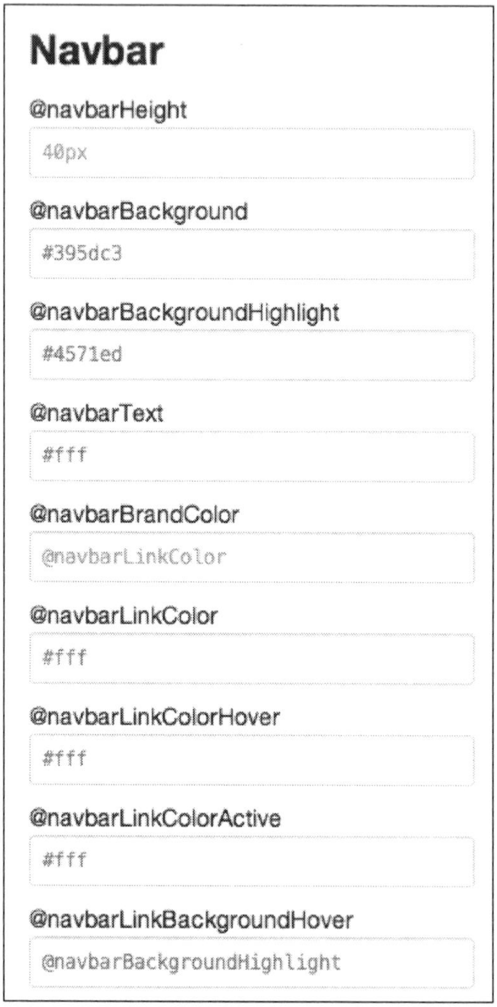

Navbar

@navbarHeight

```
40px
```

@navbarBackground

```
#395dc3
```

@navbarBackgroundHighlight

```
#4571ed
```

@navbarText

```
#fff
```

@navbarBrandColor

```
@navbarLinkColor
```

@navbarLinkColor

```
#fff
```

@navbarLinkColorHover

```
#fff
```

@navbarLinkColorActive

```
#fff
```

@navbarLinkBackgroundHover

```
@navbarBackgroundHighlight
```

7. Scroll down to the big **Customize and Download** button, and click on it. Your browser will download a new ZIP folder named `bootstrap.zip`. Extract the ZIP folder, which will give you a new folder named simply `bootstrap`. Change the folder name to `bootstrap-custom` to help you keep it straight.

8. Now move inside the newly downloaded folder. Delete the `img` folder, as the glyphicon files will be identical to what we already have.

9. Open the CSS folder to make sure that it does not contain the `error.txt` file. If it does, an error in one of the values you entered in the **Customize** page caused the CSS files not to compile properly. This could include a missing quote mark, an unnecessary semicolon, or a typo. You'll have to find and correct that, then download the file again.

10. Rename the `css` folder to `css-custom` and the `js` folder to `js-custom`. Then add "-custom" to the name of each file inside. Thus you'll have this new folder and file structure:

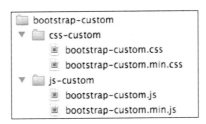

11. Copy your new custom files to the appropriate `css` and `js` folders in your Bootstrap site folder, so that they appear right alongside your current `css` and `js` files.

12. Copy your new custom CSS files to the `css` folder in your Bootstrap site. Compare the size of the new files against the originals. Here is what I found:

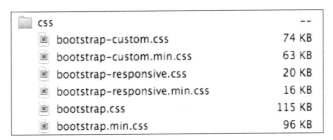

Notice that the new `bootstrap-custom.min.css` file is 35 percent smaller than the original `bootstrap.min.css`, promising much faster load times for the users.

13. Now turn to the `js` files. Copy your custom JavaScript files to the `js` folder in your Bootstrap site. Again, let's compare file size. Here is what I found:

📁 js	--
🔲 bootstrap-custom.js	19 KB
🔲 bootstrap-custom.min.js	8 KB
🔲 bootstrap.js	56 KB
🔲 bootstrap.min.js	26 KB
🔲 jquery-1.7.2.min.js	95 KB

The new `bootstrap-custom.min.js` is a mere 8 KB—less than one third the size of the original! Our customizing steps have made a big difference.

14. Now let's hook up our new files and see how they work. We're going to begin with our custom JavaScript file. Open `index.html` in your editor, and scroll down to near the closing `</body>` tag. You'll see that the current links point to the minified versions of our JavaScript files—both with jQuery and with Bootstrap's original JavaScript file. The ".min" in these files indicates the minified version.

```
<script src="js/jquery-1.7.2.min.js"></script>
<script src="js/bootstrap.min.js"></script>
```

This is good, as minification reduces file sizes and speeds up browser processing. So let's update the second link to point to the minified version of our custom file, as follows:

```
<script src="js/bootstrap-custom.min.js"></script>
```

Save the file. Then refresh the homepage in your browser. Test the navbar drop-down item to make sure it works. If it does, then your custom Bootstrap plugin is doing its job!

15. Take a minute to open all of your HTML files and update their JavaScript links to point to your new custom file in just the same way. Make it simple by copying and pasting the entire line from your `index.html` file to replace the corresponding line in each other file.

Leave your HTML files open for our next steps.

16. Now for the CSS! If you look at the stylesheet links in the head of our pages, you'll see that they point to the unminified files: `bootstrap.css` and `bootstrap-responsive.css`. Edit these lines in all of your site's HTML files to link to the minified versions of your custom CSS and the responsive CSS.

Your stylesheet links should now read as follows:

❑   `<link href="css/bootstrap-custom.min.css"`
     `rel="stylesheet">`

❑ `<link href="css/bootstrap-responsive.min.css" rel="stylesheet">`

Update these same lines throughout all of your HTML files.

17. Let's test our CSS results. Refresh your pages. They should look basically the same, except for your headings! These should now be using the Palatino font family we specified.

18. What about changes we made to the navbar? As of Bootstrap version 2.1, the customizations we made are being overridden by the styles that come with the `navbar-inverse` class. This class converts the navbar to its current dark color scheme. We could opt at this point to edit the CSS file directly. But it's simpler to simply remove the unnecessary class.

    In your index.html file, find the `div class="navbar ..."` at or near line 35. You'll see it looks like this:

    ```
    <div class="navbar navbar-inverse navbar-fixed-top">
    ```

    Delete the class navbar-inverse, so that this line now looks like this:

    ```
    <div class="navbar navbar-fixed-top">
    ```

    Save the file, refresh it in your browser, and you should see your new color scheme!

19. Update this same line in your other HTML files.

20. Save your files, refresh them in your browser, and click through your site.
    Not bad! The color scheme is not fully woven through the rest of your site.
    You may want to update the color values for buttons and dropdowns, for example.
    You're now experienced and equipped. Have a go at it!

How it works...

One of the great things about Bootstrap is that it provides CSS styles and JavaScript behaviors for all of the things we need most often in our websites. And yet, covering all the bases requires a large code base. Thus it's important—and exciting—that we can use Bootstrap's customize page as a fast and friendly way to compile custom files, trimmed down to provide just the styles and behaviors we utilize in our sites.

Meanwhile, Bootstrap's CSS is built using some powerful variables than enable us to get a running start at customizing our Bootstrap site with its own distinctive look and feel.

There's more...

Though it's beyond the scope of this brief book, you may soon want to start adding your own custom styles. You might choose to edit your `bootstrap-custom.css` file directly or add a custom stylesheet of your own. Eventually, you may want to go the whole way, download all the Bootstrap source files, and work with Bootstrap's Less files to compile your own custom CSS like a pro. The point of Bootstrap is not to lock you in. Quite the opposite, it provides many opportunities for you to bring your own creativity to bear. As with any framework, it takes some work to get familiar with the new workflow. But the effort has a payoff, as soon you'll be operating with greater efficiency and effectiveness!

Ch 5: Upload, Test & Launch

Uploading, testing, and launching (Must know)

Your first Bootstrap site is well underway. It sports a variety of content formats, laid out with a solid grid system, tied together with a user-friendly navbar, all in accord with current web standards and best practices. Custom design innovations are underway. CSS and JavaScript files have been optimized for site performance. These are signs of serious web development, and they're something to celebrate.

But before we celebrate, we need to upload and test!

Test? Isn't the point of Bootstrap to reduce headaches and conquer cross-browser compatibility issues? Do we still need to test?

Fair questions. Yes, Bootstrap's built to help. And yet, we still need to test. A community-supported framework greatly reduces headaches, but trouble can creep in at any number of points. Each version of Bootstrap fixes certain problems, even as new features run into trouble with some browsers under certain conditions. Other problems can stem from your own innovations on Bootstrap. A malformed tag may be forgiven by one browser but wreak havoc in another. Nothing can replace testing.

What's more, the right tools give us the opportunity to test Bootstrap's responsive grid and navbar, ensuring that they work as they should across devices of varying sizes, from handhelds to tablets to widescreens. Many of these tools require our site to be online.

So let's upload our site, run it through its paces, make adjustments if necessary, and then launch!

Getting ready

I'm going to assume you have web hosting with FTP access, an FTP client, and some experience putting files online. If you don't have these things or need some help with them, now would be a great time to get those arranged. Then come back!

In the testing phase, I'm going to reference two online services:

- **Adobe BrowserLab**: This is free with an Adobe ID (registration required). Visit `https://browserlab.adobe.com/`.

- **BrowserStack**: The free trial available (registration required)—a 30 minute limit, so don't sign up until ready! You can sign up for a free trial from `http://www.browserstack.com`.

These services meet the present need well. Feel free to check them out for yourself. I'll reference them in what follows. If you are aware of better services, or have access to a physical lab of testing devices, feel free to use them!

How to do it...

1. Prior to taking it online, we need to double-check to ensure everything works as it should. From its current location on your local computer, open `index.html` in a browser and click through the site one more time to make sure everything is working.

2. This is optional. You might choose to create a `robots.txt` file to tell search engines not to pay attention to your test site. If search engines start indexing your test site, this can create hassles for tracking your website analytics later. If you'd like to protect against this, create a new file in your code editor. Save it in your main site directly, right next to your HTML files, with the filename `robots.txt`. Enter the following lines in the content of this file:

    ```
    User-agent: *
    Disallow: /
    ```

    The first line uses the wild card to address all search engines. The second line requests that the search engine avoid indexing any and all directories of the site.

    Save the file.

3. Using your web hosting provider's panel tools or your FTP client, create a directory for testing your site. This might be a subfolder or subdomain of your main site's future location. Your might choose to name the location in a relatively obscure way to reduce the chances that random users will stumble across it. (You could choose to password protect the directory, but this could make our testing steps more complicated.)

4. Using your FTP client, upload your site files to your test location. You might choose to exclude the `_Carousel Images` folder as we've moved our production images to the `img` folder. (If you created the `robots.txt` file, include it as well.)

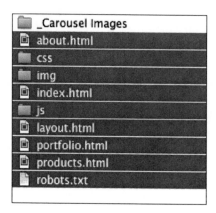

Once the transfer is complete, you should see your files online in your FTP browser.

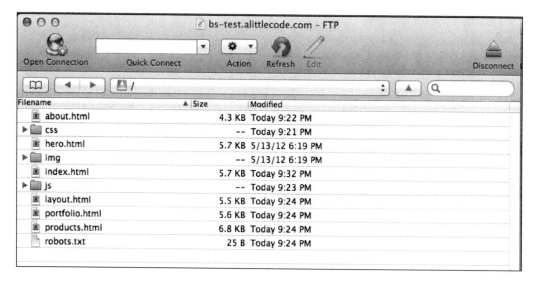

5.   Now navigate to this directory in your browser. If you've gotten it right, you should be duly rewarded:

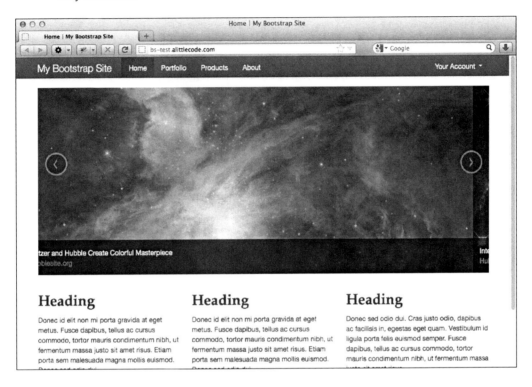

Congratulations! You're online! We're ready for testing.

There are many tools to help with testing major desktop browsers. One of these is Adobe's free Browser Lab, which requires a free registration. In your favorite browser, navigate to Adobe BrowserLab: `http://browserlab.adobe.com/`.

Click on **Start using Adobe BrowserLab**, sign in, and provide the URL for your test site. BrowserLab will start loading screenshots of how your site looks across major browsers and operating systems. Click through the options to see your results.

You may notice that many site elements look basically the same across various browsers, with some minor differences. Because Bootstrap follows the principle of progressive enhancement, you should find that major features of design and layout, JavaScript behaviors, and fundamental usability considerations remain consistent across browsers. A few fine details may change. Some older browsers, for example, will not render Bootstrap's CSS3 gradients or rounded corners. Thus, the buttons, navbar, and carousel handles may look somewhat different across these browsers.

But these elements remain obvious and easy to use. For example, the handles for moving to the next and previous items in the slideshow are square (see the following screenshot), and yet they are clearly visible and usable.

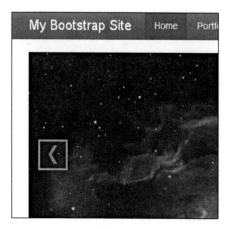

Likewise, buttons lack rounded corners in Internet Explorer 8. Again, this is not a large loss. There is no impact upon fundamentals of usability. Our site works great in older browsers. It works even better in modern browsers. This is progressive enhancement in action.

If your results are like mine, you will see that your site performs well across major browsers in both OS X and Windows, including Internet Explorer 7. (Internet Explorer 6 is not supported.)

If you run into problems, you may want to double check your code, run W3 validation on your HTML and CSS files (always a good idea anyway), and then consult resources such as those listed in the appendix in this book to see if anyone else is reporting a similar problem.

If your results are like mine, congratulations!

Time to test for mobile devices. If you're like me, you may own a phone, a tablet, and/or another mobile device. You may aspire to collect more devices, so that you may conduct adequate testing across major mobile platforms (iOS and Android as the current leaders), but you haven't yet accumulated very many. If that's your situation, you may want to try a service such as BrowserShots. Much like Adobe's service, BrowserShots provides the ability to discover how your site performs across many industry leading browsers. In the case of BrowserShots, this includes a plethora of mobile browsers and devices.

If you'd like to try it, set aside 30 minutes to work straight, sign up for a free BrowserShots trial, enter your URL and start testing! Again, I found that my site performed very well across all major devices.

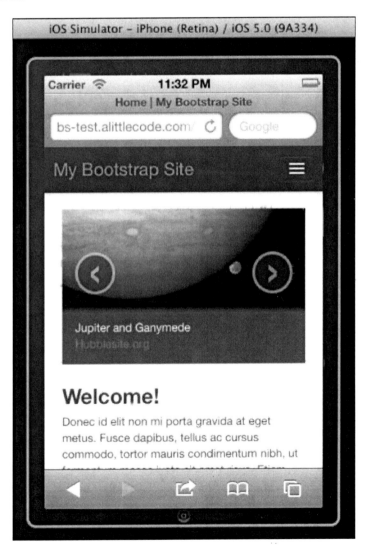

Problems occasionally appear, however. When they do, I recommend consulting the resources listed in the *Appendix: Bootstrap resources* section of this book.

If your results are like mine—congratulations! You can consider your site tested and ready for production.

Time to launch! You can move your site files from their temporary test location to the main directory where you want your site to be hosted.

If you want your site to be indexed by and ranked in search engines, you'll need to edit the `robots.txt` file. Open it in your editor. Delete the forward slash from the second line, so that the file contents read as follows:

```
User-agent: *
Disallow:
```

That's it—remove the slash from the second line. This allows search engines to index all files and folders of your website, helping users find their way to your pages.

Time to celebrate!

There's more...

Take some time to enjoy the moment. Give yourself a pat on the back.

But don't be satisfied! Not yet. This is just the beginning of great things to come. Now to keep growing. There's much to learn, and much more to do. Check out the *Appendix: Bootstrap resources* section for some excellent resources to speed you on your way!

Appendix: Bootstrap resources

The following resources will help speed you on your way to greater freedom and confidence with Twitter Bootstrap:

- ▸ Twitter Bootstrap homepage and documentation (`http://twitter.github.com/bootstrap/`): This is the best and most reliable resource. Always check here first!

- ▸ The Twitter Bootstrap GitHub project page (`https://github.com/twitter/bootstrap/`): Essential resources for the Bootstrap development community.

- ▸ The Bootstrap blog (`http://blog.getbootstrap.com/`): Stay abreast of official statements and updates from lead developers.

- ▸ Follow Twitter Bootstrap (@twbootstrap) on Twitter (`https://twitter.com/twbootstrap/`): An indispensable way to stay informed.

- ▸ The Bootstrap Google Group (`http://groups.google.com/group/twitter-bootstrap/`): A great place to ask questions and request assistance.

- ▸ Stack overflow (`http://stackoverflow.com/`): A fantastic support community, with an extensive Twitter Bootstrap section: `http://stackoverflow.com/questions/tagged/twitter-bootstrap`.

- ▸ Targeted web searches: Want help customizing your color scheme? Try searching "Twitter Bootstrap custom color scheme". Want to integrate jQuery form validation? Try "Twitter Bootstrap jQuery form validation". And so on. You get the idea.

Thank you for buying
Twitter Bootstrap Web Development How-To

About Packt Publishing

Packt, pronounced 'packed', published its first book *"Mastering phpMyAdmin for Effective MySQL Management"* in April 2004 and subsequently continued to specialize in publishing highly focused books on specific technologies and solutions.

Our books and publications share the experiences of your fellow IT professionals in adapting and customizing today's systems, applications, and frameworks. Our solution based books give you the knowledge and power to customize the software and technologies you're using to get the job done. Packt books are more specific and less general than the IT books you have seen in the past. Our unique business model allows us to bring you more focused information, giving you more of what you need to know, and less of what you don't.

Packt is a modern, yet unique publishing company, which focuses on producing quality, cutting-edge books for communities of developers, administrators, and newbies alike. For more information, please visit our website: www.packtpub.com.

About Packt Open Source

In 2010, Packt launched two new brands, Packt Open Source and Packt Enterprise, in order to continue its focus on specialization. This book is part of the Packt Open Source brand, home to books published on software built around Open Source licences, and offering information to anybody from advanced developers to budding web designers. The Open Source brand also runs Packt's Open Source Royalty Scheme, by which Packt gives a royalty to each Open Source project about whose software a book is sold.

Writing for Packt

We welcome all inquiries from people who are interested in authoring. Book proposals should be sent to author@packtpub.com. If your book idea is still at an early stage and you would like to discuss it first before writing a formal book proposal, contact us; one of our commissioning editors will get in touch with you.

We're not just looking for published authors; if you have strong technical skills but no writing experience, our experienced editors can help you develop a writing career, or simply get some additional reward for your expertise.

open source
community experience distilled

HTML5 Boilerplate Web
Development

HTML5 Boilerplate Web Development

ISBN: 978-1-84951-850-5   Paperback: 144 pages

Master HTML5 Boilerplate web development with a
robust set of templates to get your web projects done
quickly and effectively.

1. Master HTML5 Boilerplate as starting templates
    for future projects

2. Learn how to optimize your workflow with
    HTML5 Boilerplate templates and set up servers
    optimized for performance

3. Learn to feature-detect and serve appropriate
    styles and scripts across browser types

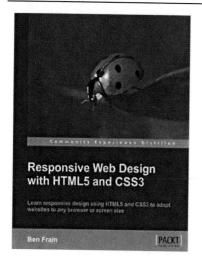

Responsive Web Design
with HTML5 and CSS3

**Responsive Web Design with
HTML5 and CSS3**

ISBN: 978-1-84969-318-9   Paperback: 324 pages

Learn responsive design using HTML5 and CSS3 to
adapt websites to any browser or screen size

1. Everything needed to code websites in HTML5
    and CSS3 that are responsive to every device or
    screen size

2. Learn the main new features of HTML5 and
    use CSS3's stunning new capabilities including
    animations, transitions and transformations

3. Real world examples show how to progressively
    enhance a responsive design while providing fall
    backs for older browsers

Please check **www.PacktPub.com** for information on our titles

Dreamweaver CS5.5 Mobile and Web Development with HTML5, CSS3, and jQuery

ISBN: 978-1-84969-158-1   Paperback: 284 pages

Harness the cutting edge features of Dreamweaver for mobile and web development

1. Create web pages in Dreamweaver using the latest technology and approach

2. Add multimedia and interactivity to your websites

3. Optimize your websites for a wide range of platforms and build mobile apps with Dreamweaver

4. A practical guide filled with many examples for making the best use of Dreamweaver's latest features

CouchDB and PHP Web Development Beginner's Guide

ISBN: 978-1-84951-358-6   Paperback: 304 pages

Get your PHP application from conception to deployment by leveraging CouchDB's robust features

1. Build and deploy a flexible Social Networking application using PHP and leveraging key features of CouchDB to do the heavy lifting

2. Explore the features and functionality of CouchDB, by taking a deep look into Documents, Views, Replication, and much more.

3. Conceptualize a lightweight PHP framework from scratch and write code that can easily port to other frameworks

Please check **www.PacktPub.com** for information on our titles

CPSIA information can be obtained at www.ICGtesting.com
Printed in the USA
BVOW061421071212

307529BV00003B/113/P